# THE CROW'S VOW

# The Crow's Vow

### SUSAN BRISCOE

SIGNAL EDITIONS IS AN IMPRINT OF VÉHICULE PRESS

Published with the generous assistance of The Canada Council for the Arts and the Book Publishing Industry Development Program of the Department of Canadian Heritage and the Société de développement des entreprises culturelles du Québec (SODEC).

SIGNAL EDITIONS EDITOR: CARMINE STARNINO

Cover design: David Drummond
Photo of author: Oliver Philbin-Briscoe
Set in Filosofia and Minion by Simon Garamond
Printed by Marquis Book Printing Inc.

LIBRARY AND ARCHIVES CANADA CATALOGUING IN PUBLICATION

Briscoe, Susan
The Crow's Vow / Susan Briscoe.
Poems.
ISBN: 978-1-55065-287-1
I . Title.

PS8603.R565C76 2010     C811'.6     C2010-900774-3


Published by Véhicule Press, Montréal, Québec, Canada
www.vehiculepress.com

Distribution in Canada by LitDistCo
www.litdistco.ca

Distributed in the U.S. by Independent Publishers Group
www.ipgbook.com


Printed in Canada on 100% post-consumer recycled paper.

*for Martin*

# Acknowledgements

Some of these poems have previously appeared, some in different forms, in *Maisonneuve*, *The Antigonish Review*, and in *Sprung*, a Tibbits Hill Press chapbook.

I would like to thank several poets who were, in various ways, crucial to the conception and completion of this manuscript: the late Rob Allen, whose long poem workshop got me started with this project; Stephanie Bolster, a wonderful teacher, for encouraging me to continue with these poems; Carmine Starnino, for his insistence that I do better; and Antony Di Nardo, for the solace of his literary friendship. Thanks also go to Michael Harris, my earliest mentor.

I would also like to express my gratitude to my parents for their support and to my friends and family for their kindness. Special acknowledgements are also due to my children for their tolerance and self-reliance, and to my husband, for being there still.

# Contents

# Winter into Spring

An icy mist,
no mountains this morning.

The world is a smaller circle.
Look closer:

ribbons of deer tracks
strung across the snow

and three brown apples
that never fell.

Your traps
all along the edges.

Spring
in the subtlest colours of winter:

faint pink of maple,
gold tinge of birch,

yet spruce almost black
against the whitest greys.

We wake to a field mouse,
soft brown fur and clean white belly.

I could skin the whole family,
stitch pretty mittens.

So cold the house cracks
loud as solid lake. Deer

in the morning dark,
huddled at the cedar; they must eat

or freeze. Seems impossible
their cloven hooves don't

draw the ice up into their bones,
still their hearts. How do I not

find chickadees, scattered, hard
as marbles, on the snow?

Last night in the moonlight,
the shadow of smoke on snow

and coyotes, nearer this time,
their rising cries.

If I am very careful,
I can trace an arc across the sky,

know how something begins
and ends. Watch the moon set,

turn, wait for the sun
on the other side.

Flood of dreams,
as if finally

a dam broke.
You have been pulling the stones for months—

thought I wouldn't notice,
but I knew,

waited for the slow crash,
the rush to wash me clean, or away.

Wake downstream and wet,
wade, stumblingly, back.

I've not pockets enough
for all this. Had grown used

to a frugal life: kisses
like slim dimes slipped

into a click-shut purse;
notes of promise

worn thin as lint.
With you

I pull out every pot and bowl,
fill them all to spilling.

Kitchen tulips too red,
daffodils too yellow

in this horizontal light. A dream
of our blue crystal shattering

at my touch. Dry air snaps with static,
dissatisfaction.

I scribble a self-portrait
in orange crayon,

trace an outline of you
that won't fit the page.

Satie's black lines on white,
songs like winter forms.

A small snow shrinks the landscape;
its falling fills minutes.

Three crows hold still
so long

they wear bridal cloaks.
It has been cold,

but here,
a *petite ouverture à danser.*

Clouds hunker
upon the mountain.

I contemplate the woodpile,
its promise of warmth.

While you sleep I hold my hand near,
compare your heat.

The snow melts first
at the base of things,

large stones, trees,
fence posts.

A fox runs across the yard,
across the street and another yard.

Winter-thin
and shabby in her red furs,

she whisks her tail
and tosses her head, chasing

the glitter of sunlight on spring snow.
Oh, she is on fire—

so alive!
Every tip of fur alive.

A south wind ripped limbs
from trees during the night,

the fresh wounds pale
against dark, wet bark.

Tatters of leaves,
empty seed stalks rattle.

Broken bones of the garden exposed,
stones like scattered teeth.

A new snow lays a clean sheet
over the remains.

The streams are running again
after a night of rain,

flowing around slabs of ice,
their stilled selves.

A drawing exercise: negative shapes.
What is left unsaid

becomes an affirmation. A cracked sky
for branch and twig.

A ghost of you
erasing the chair.

We have learned nothing
from the songbirds.

You have brought me shiny bits
and baubles, a crow's cache

of electronics and appliances, things
with instructions in six scripts.

Chainsaw, lawnmower. Winter tires
and summer too. In fact the whole car.

But not once have you danced,
and I have yet to hear you sing.

The crows decide:
it's time to nest.

There is some argument over this.
Perhaps over site, or materials. Perhaps, even,

over mates. But they will settle down soon
to brood over clutches,

give up their morning gossip
for another imperative.

Because they too don't sing,
I listen.

Overnight
the grass is green,

the hills eased
into a hazy blue.

It's warm enough for mating:
birds pour notes

from wide throats,
roll round vowel sounds.

The bedroom window
open.

Five a.m. and whole flocks in concert.
A sudden hush over the birds:

Snow. This winter is relentless.
Across the pasture, pale green

glances through the falling veil.
And already

next year's firewood,
dumped in the yard.

Our day's work,
to stack, make order.

Spring into Summer

I must teach you
to buttress the rows:

yesterday's work undone
in a slow collapse,

a cascade of split logs
rejecting the tension

of near-balance.
There is more rest in their sprawl,

the resumption of chaos. You
resist, want this to be easier.

There is no echo
of slammed door. No, you slip out so quietly

the courting cardinals, whose songs I attend,
never falter: the transcription is intact

Yet the rattling in my skull
builds to a dense thrum. Louder

than the dump trucks carting away the hills.
An accumulation,

each small catching of latch.
It incapacitates.

You'd expect a resurrection of sorts.
What with daffodils and forsythia

trumpeting their loudest yellows, a ruckus
of jays in the yard.

But the top of the mountain is still dark
with winter. Green

creeps slowly up the north slope.
I measure its progress across days,

weeks, thinking of gifts offered
that I've failed to receive.

Rings that rattled loose,
knocking between knuckles,

have tightened again, resist
this twisting off. I watch them

from across the kitchen,
their passive intersecting circles.

Bare,
my hands consider,

reconsider. Touch,
the most familiar things.

Spring has spilled
its most beguiling perfumes

— honeysuckle, lilac,
lily of the valley —

all at once, luring me
down to a clover bed

to breathe in,
in, with you if you would,

while the apple tree swings
its hips and hums.

The meadow grass sings
of the long-drained sea, courting

the night sky with its tiny star flowers.
Harbouring wild blooms too modest

or wayward
for the kept beds,

it whispers palimpsest lists
of unremembered names,

a reminder of endearments
we have dropped.

How quickly our work is consumed;
diligently edged beds

undefined by elastic-rooted sorrel
or sideways spikes of twitch grass.

My fault the self-sown mallow,
the violets and purple vetch—

all too pretty to pull.
And oh,

the possibility of strawberries
from the wild runners!

Not only the moon but the stars too,
these hand-fasting rings.

The first a promise pulled from the sky
and tied to my hand like a balloon—

lovelorn ghost, luminous and round.
The second a circle

of workaday vows plucked
from a universe of needs

and fixed
for the ordinary orbit of years.

Yours a band like the milky way
wrapped around a finger, its even gleam

my reminder: I am the one thing
you have to love you.

When our honeymoon hands lay idle of work,
we measured segments

from knuckle to knuckle, pressed
each pink pad against another.

You held my fist until it opened.
I turned your hand, cupped, full.

For you: a birdfeeder
to hang in the dead sumac.

Soon they are flying in perfect arcs,
streamers

from tree to tree.
Birds in primary colours

—cardinal, finch, and jay—
bedeck the yard,

drop feathers
like invitations.

Harder to name
are the speckled browns

and humble greys,
the various blackbirds.

Sparrows and such. Grackle,
I read once, in a poem.

Catbird I've looked up;
imagine the unlikely coupling,

hunter and hunted
locked.

We wake tired
from a night of lights;

fireflies and fireworks,
lightning, shooting stars.

A full moon
like the neighbour's floodlights,

shining into windows, into eyes.
It peered into the dark

of our small skulls,
didn't flinch.

The sun lobs great gobs
of sunshine, huge fistfuls

aimed at the good dads throwing
baseballs, tossing babies,

chasing bikes and strollers,
the weekend wheels whirling,

spinning through Saturday, Sunday—
the sun, the dads with little satellites

hurling yellow all around,
blinding us, knocking us down.

Oh, your furious daughter! And a son out of orbit,
their mother mooning around her Mars—

Between this calamitous reconstellation
and my latest unfinished essay,

*Diversion, Inversion, and Perversion: Sexual
and Textual Subversive Strategies Against the Discomfort*

*of Dichotomy in Ross, Cohen, and Engel,* no wonder
you have fled, head spinning,

to the city, rented an apartment far too small
for us all.

Pinned to the pillow:
*You are loved.* Okay,

but enough? Dangling
from the birch, a certain leaf says *sorry.*

I could pluck it, slip it amongst your socks.
Another says *don't go*. But there—

*Fuck You* waves its guiltless green.
The tree rustles a thousand leaves,

all the possible paper notes,
words for endings, or continuings.

Another note:
*feed the birds.*

The landscape a monochrome,
green wash over everything;

nothing to paint
after all this rain.

Scoop black seeds
into the feeder;

sunflower sprouts
on the ground where they've dropped.

# Summer into Fall

The crows are a nuisance at this hour.
I am coming to know their caws,

their serious dramas.
The one with the broken voice box,

their outrage at the cats. Proprietary swoops
across the yard. They're not peripheral creatures

like deer who linger at edges.
All night I've held to my side, wished

a forgetful arm around my waist,
if only to shrug it off.

Under the willow, mulling
over who loves

or is unloved. A nuthatch
so near it startles

at my gaze. Glossed eye
dark as a beetle grub unearthed.

Yours of sky after rain.
It's the wrong question, I know.

In these silvering leaves are answers,
but we can't figure out what to ask.

There's a hole in the yard.
Yesterday I wielded the spade,

dug at it some more. Eyed its depth,
paced its span. Satisfying work.

A robin watched from the swing set.
My boy, now and then, stood by:

there are things he could do with a hole this size.
Every day of your absence I dig.

If you don't come soon
the garden will be gone.

Certainly, this is not
the way it is done.

The distance between each side
of our marital bed reaches

a hundred thousand metres,
from baked urban brick

to cool Appalachian wood,
across every binary we could think of.

Saboteurs, we two, stretching our tenuous bond
like my boys their elastics, aimed at the eyes.

The late, awaited summer
swaggers in,

a curtain call without the play. Dazzled,
the garden drinks

the sun like liquid, undiluted.
The asparagus thrusts new shoots,

the magnolia opens new blooms. But heat trips us
into irritation beyond an itch—

a rash of hives. Bouquet of stinging nettles,
wild rose, and water lilies dripping mud from the pond.

Your complaint:
invisibility. It *is* hard to see you

across the hectares of corn leeching
the lowlands between this hill

and the city squatting in its river—I argue, just to win.
Were I honest, I'd admit to being deaf

as well as blind. We have become abstractions.
A theory of opposites. Or, a conversation

looped back on itself, the half-twisted telephone wire
a Möbius strip.

We pass each other on the bridge,
commuting in contrary streams of traffic.

This seems an incident of portent,
a moment of unexpected recognition,

our exuberant waving. We reach
for cell phones, but what is there to say?

It's already over, our back-to-back distance
increasing exponentially,

that fleeting nearness
a rear-view gaze already lost.

Headache and the usual doubt,
an attempt to sleep in.

Nothing will get done
but a listless shifting between tasks,

a book opened but turned over.
Don't look at the dulling green,

the muted blue of the hills.
Better set an easel, paint instead

a bowl or vase, something
to hold something from this lost day.

The coyotes are coming down from the mountains
where the hunting has grown thin.

They set the valley dogs to barking, hard monotones
like stones the size for throwing.

Last year they got the cats, fattened
on a daily breakfast of birds. Their ambush

devised, practised, refined.
The clever executions:

hard shakes, snapped necks.
A quick dispatch, and clean.

The equinox: you insist
it's my turn to visit, believe equal measures

will balance all our opposites. Ever the Libra,
my lover of ideals.

Three dark omens:
the midnight cawing of a crow;

a beggar —fat, black-clad, red-eyed woman—
who accepted the burger, laughed at my back;

and a bad-luck black cat who darted in front of the car,
danced a sick jig with its broken leg.

Unfamiliar birds in the yard. They know a time of want
is coming, steal food from each other's mouths.

We've been obstinate in our lessons.
Don't listen. Balk

at explanation, repetition, examination.
"You're smart; this shouldn't be hard."

But it is, or I'm not. I argue answers given, patiently
or not. Withhold

the golden star. Now you've turned truant,
switched June for September.

A fog,
but somehow

the sun shines through it,
finds the yellow in every leaf.

The crows are bossing us all up
but the other birds are quiet,

contemplative now.
Or, disquiet.

Perhaps
they have flown already.

I can hear the geese call
constant encouragement to each other,

winter at their tails,
but my eye

is slow to find its focus
in a sky as blankly blue

as cerulean from the tube.
What comfort the unquestioned

necessity would be,
but we are silenced by too many needs.

The limbs can't hold them all,
past ripe. Dropped,

apples roll down the hill,
gathering bruises. Fill the ditches

with sweet rot
to get the skunks and racoons

Friday-night drunk. Not that we
would have eaten after the disfiguring worms:

you buy a bag of perfect apples,
and we don't have any fun.

We're in the storage room again.
I sit on luggage lumpy with some big-eyed child,

stack bags packed with celibacy
—*don't unzip!*

Your crates are taped, gimpy father
like a pugilist jack-in-the-box

under button-downs, laundered, pink and pale blue.
We've been through it all before,

but still we sift through, note contents,
lock the door when we leave.

Empty,
the feeder swings in wild arcs,

the plaything of an errant east wind
that's knocked out all the seed.

The jays and chickadees
approach, reproach.

Perched on the sumac,
they lean into gusts,

consider the alternatives,
to forage or wait.

# Fall into Winter

Cold, bare-handed work,
fingers rooting

for old rhizomes and bulbs.
White tentacles disentangled,

divided, replanted. Spring's
sun-tipped flowers turned broody, inward:

irises are pale crustaceans,
the hyacinth a scrotal half.

Mallow's taproot, spine-like, persistent,
has drilled deeper than I can dig.

Slow sap drawn
into a single stem,

a November rose opens
to the wan sun.

How much nobler, it seems,
than summer's easy profusions

whose fresh petals fell,
filling our hands. Still,

you think I should want more
than just this.

The moon slipped
into an envelope of sky.

In the dimmest light of dawn
I can't see the lines

but draw anyway—
don't want the lamp turning windows

into mirrors.
The sun's nearing reveals

these arcs as parts of spirals;
there are no closed circles.

The tamarack
knows its moment:

a background of woods brown,
an umber warmed, not burnt,

and the hills behind near black.
The skies weighing heavy

to break, leak
a slant illumination.

And then
the yellow blazes—

I bring them all in,
relics of fertility:

brittle twists of sweet pea pods and
pepper-shaker poppies, all shaken;

Fibonacci swirls of pinecone,
and other things to count.

Sumac plumes remember
flaring red

from limb tips,
how birds flocked.

Broken fences—
boards splintered like snapped bones;

chain link crumpled, kicked in the gut;
and posts, looking to rest, leaning

against nothing. Then a horse running crazy,
gate smashed. We startle each other

on the stony road, caught
in a thin snare of sight. Wild-eyed,

it wheels away, running unsure,
fences again beyond.

Driving south, the road ahead
too clear, straight,

its beacon sun. How easy
to not turn back, to speed

towards the border I can cross
with any fib. They would not ask

what I left behind: half-grown children,
the latest to-do list, you, the spaghetti pot unwashed—

me, that woman, her stories unfinished.
The road ahead so clear.

A bloated, belly-up frog of a moon
floats out from the underworld, dragging

its sallow beam across wind-scraped snow.
It is following me home,

weaving like a drunk
from one side of the highway

to the other. When you call (as you always do)
to remind me of your love (because of course

I've forgotten again) it is at the top of the sky,
shimmering in skimmed-milk virtue.

A decade after my divorce,
the first Christmas card

is always from my lawyer.
A likely repeat client, she must figure.

Elegant, expensive,
I stand it on the mantle, hail

the season of peace and love.
You object, of course;

can't accept that not every gift
will be exactly what we always wanted.

I shovel the driveway,
clear a space for your arrival.

Anticipation is the unsullied snow,
sparkling its defiance of subtler sentiment.

But impatience builds with the snowbanks, scrapes
against the icy ruts. I could get out the sledgehammer,

some tool of sufficient heft,
a blunt but cutting edge,

and chip resentfully to the gravel,
glancing down the road.

Floor and table, horizontal
planes intervening

against gravity, accepting always.
Vertical blank of wall

repulsing all but the most pointed
advance of nail or hook.

Curve of bowl holding close
unless upset.

Yesterday you were the bowl. Today
I am the table, you the wall.

Horizon, first line drawn against the dark,
divides mountain

from sky.
Soon the stars will blink out,

the last to mark night's end.
But they persist, even as three crows wake,

flap from dense fir to cross a grey sky.
Even unseen, stars shift

to the west, the whole world
sliding sideways.

Your back to me,
the line of mountain.

A scarlet sun pinched out
by bands of iron cloud.

They win too easily. Hard,
red-knuckled rain will rub out the snow,

remind us that the humblest plants
— heart's ease, thyme —

are evergreen. Winter,
a breath held.

If I look at you, what will I see?
Not conflagration of maple,

nor self-absorbed little brook
muttering through undergrowth.

Maybe the hummingbird,
though you are not so fierce.

Ink spills, a blot
blooming over these creeping lines.

Words erased
in paper turned black.

Finally, disappearing,
I see you.

Not metaphor or memory or the mirage of word.
Just a man.

Now the solstice sun
leans low, reaches in

to pull long shadows, bleached streaks
across the floor. Touches insides,

undersides. Leads the gaze away from itself,
illuminates, recedes.

Still night in the morning, you
still beside me.

Snow banked to the eaves,
the driveway diminished

to the length and width of one car,
one door slightly open.

The path to the house
is of snow

packed by our boot prints,
single file.

Signal
EDITIONS

Carmine Starnino, Editor
Michael Harris, Founding Editor

THE RHINO GATE POEMS George Ellenbogen
SHADOW CABINET Richard Sanger
MAP OF DREAMS Ricardo Sternberg
THE NEW WORLD Carmine Starnino
THE LONG COLD GREEN EVENINGS OF SPRING Elisabeth Harvor
FAULT LINE Laura Lush
WHITE STONE: THE ALICE POEMS Stephanie Bolster
KEEP IT ALL Yves Boisvert (Translated by Judith Cowan)
THE GREEN ALEMBIC Louise Fabiani
THE ISLAND IN WINTER Terence Young
A TINKERS' PICNIC Peter Richardson
SARACEN ISLAND: THE POEMS OF ANDREAS KARAVIS David Solway
BEAUTIES ON MAD RIVER: SELECTED AND NEW POEMS Jan Conn
WIND AND ROOT Brent MacLaine
HISTORIES Andrew Steinmetz
ARABY Eric Ormsby
WORDS THAT WALK IN THE NIGHT Pierre Morency
    (Translated by Lissa Cowan and René Brisebois)
A PICNIC ON ICE: SELECTED POEMS Matthew Sweeney
HELIX: NEW AND SELECTED POEMS John Steffler
HERESIES: THE COMPLETE POEMS OF ANNE WILKINSON, 1924-1961
    Edited by Dean Irvine
CALLING HOME Richard Sanger
FIELDER'S CHOICE Elise Partridge
MERRYBEGOT Mary Dalton
MOUNTAIN TEA Peter Van Toorn
AN ABC OF BELLY WORK Peter Richardson
RUNNING IN PROSPECT CEMETERY Susan Glickman
MIRABEL Pierre Nepveu (Translated by Judith Cowan)
POSTSCRIPT Geoffrey Cook
STANDING WAVE Robert Allen
THERE, THERE Patrick Warner
HOW WE ALL SWIFTLY: THE FIRST SIX BOOKS Don Coles
THE NEW CANON: AN ANTHOLOGY OF CANADIAN POETRY
    Edited by Carmine Starnino
OUT TO DRY IN CAPE BRETON Anita Lahey
RED LEDGER Mary Dalton
REACHING FOR CLEAR David Solway
OX Christopher Patton
THE MECHANICAL BIRD Asa Boxer
SYMPATHY FOR THE COURIERS Peter Richardson
MORNING GOTHIC: NEW AND SELECTED POEMS George Ellenbogen
36 CORNELIAN AVENUE Christopher Wiseman
THE EMPIRE'S MISSING LINKS Walid Bitar
PENNY DREADFUL Shannon Stewart
THE STREAM EXPOSED WITH ALL ITS STONES D.G. Jones
PURE PRODUCT Jason Guriel
ANIMALS OF MY OWN KIND Harry Thurston
BOXING THE COMPASS Richard Greene
CIRCUS Michael Harris
THE CROW'S VOW Susan Briscoe

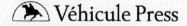 Véhicule Press